AF491202

THE IMJIN WAR

1592 Japan's Invasion of Korea

Historical Horizons

Historical Horizons

Copyright © 2023 Historical Horizons

All rights reserved

The characters and events portrayed in this book are fictitious. Any similarity to real persons, living or dead, is coincidental and not intended by the author.

No part of this book may be reproduced, or stored in a retrieval system, or transmitted in any form or by any means, electronic, mechanical, photocopying, recording, or otherwise, without express written permission of the publisher.

ISBN : 9798374005868

Cover design by: Art Painter
Library of Congress Control Number: 2018675309
Printed in the United States of America

CONTENTS

INTRODUCTION

The Imjin War, also known as the Seven-Year War, was a defining moment in the history of East Asia. Spanning from 1592 to 1598, this conflict saw the powerful Japanese warlord Toyotomi Hideyoshi launch a massive invasion of the Korean Peninsula, with the ultimate goal of conquering China and the Ming Dynasty. The war was marked by brutal battles and atrocities committed by both sides, and its impact was felt for decades to come. This book will delve into the causes, events, and aftermath of the Imjin War, providing a comprehensive look at one of the most significant conflicts of the late 16th century. From the strategies and tactics of the warring armies to the political machinations of the leaders involved, readers will gain a deeper understanding of the events that shaped the history of East Asia. With the use of primary sources and latest historical research, this book will give a full account of the Imjin War, and its continuing significance in the region today.

PROLOGUE

The Imjin War, also known as the Seven Year War, was one of the most significant conflicts in East Asian history. Spanning from 1592 to 1598, this war was fought between the Joseon dynasty of Korea and the invading armies of Japan's Toyotomi Hideyoshi. The war would have far-reaching consequences for all three nations involved, shaping the political and cultural landscape for centuries to come.

For the Koreans, the Imjin War was a time of immense suffering and sacrifice. The people of the Joseon dynasty were not prepared for the scale of the Japanese invasion and were quickly overrun by the well-trained and well-equipped Japanese armies. Entire cities were laid to waste, and tens of thousands of innocent civilians were killed or taken as prisoners.

Despite the overwhelming odds against them, the Koreans fought bravely and tenaciously. One of the most notable figures of this conflict is Admiral Yi Sun-shin, who with a small fleet of 13 ships managed to defeat the much larger Japanese naval forces and turn the tide of the war in favor of the Koreans.

For the Japanese, the Imjin War was a costly and ultimately futile endeavor. Hideyoshi's dream of conquering Korea and China was never realized, and the war drained the resources of many powerful daimyos. The war also marked the beginning of the end for the Toyotomi dynasty, as powerful lords like Tokugawa Ieyasu began to consolidate their power and challenge Hideyoshi's rule.

The Imjin War also had a significant impact on the Ming dynasty of China, who came to the aid of the Koreans and fought several major battles against the Japanese. The war weakened the Ming, making them vulnerable to the Manchu invasions that would ultimately lead to the collapse of the dynasty in 1644.

This book aims to provide a comprehensive and in-depth look at the Imjin War, from the causes and motivations of the war to the key battles and figures that shaped its outcome. We will explore the impact of the war on the people of Korea, Japan, and China and how it shaped the political and cultural landscape of East Asia for centuries to come.

JAPAN'S NEW CHALLENGES

In the 17th century, Japan was beginning a new era as the country had recently been united, ending the Sengoku Jidai period of warfare. However, peace presented a new challenge for Toyotomi Hideyoshi, the new overlord, as there were now hundreds of thousands of warriors with no war to fight. To address this, Hideyoshi turned his ambitions outward and, using some of the most experienced armies in Japanese history, launched an invasion of Korea.

HIDEYOSHI'S FAILED INVASION OF KOREA

Diplomatic and Tragic Outcome 1587-1590

In 1582, Toyotomi Hideyoshi, succeeded his master Oda Nobunaga and claimed control of Honshu. He quickly subdued Shikoku in 1585 and Kyushu in 1587, bringing Japan closer to unification. Hideyoshi allowed rival daimyos who swore allegiance to him to keep their territories and promised them more lands and spoils. However, once Japan was unified, there would be no more battles to fight or gains to be had. To address this, he began to make plans to turn his vassals outwards in the late 1580s and set his sights on Korea as the initial target and the Chinese Ming Empire as the next step.

These invasion plans were not only a way to keep his war-like vassals busy, but also a reflection of Hideyoshi's belief that his power should extend beyond the confines of Japan. He was convinced that his destiny was to conquer further afield, just like Nobunaga before him.

One of Hideyoshi's most recent conquests was the island of Tsushima, located at the midpoint of the Tsushima Strait. The lords of the Sō clan, which controlled the island, had become Hideyoshi's vassals and were ordered to deliver a message to the Koreans demanding their submission to the Japanese state. This put the Sō clan in a difficult position as their long-standing relations with the Korean Joseon monarchy made them ideal diplomats, but an outbreak of hostilities between Korea and Japan would damage the trade that provided the clan with much of its wealth.

Aiming to soften the diplomatic blow as much as he could, Sō Yoshishige altered Hideyoshi's message to the Korean court, blunting much of its threats and demands, and changing it so that it stipulated only a simple tribute mission be sent to Japan in order to confirm Korea's respect. However, this plan would backfire. In a lethal blunder, the Sō clan leader sent a rough, hardened subordinate known as Yutani Yasuhiro to deliver the message, instead of going himself. Yasuhiro conducted himself in the most indelicate way possible, insulting his Korean hosts by degrading the size of their spears compared to the Japanese, and mocking their lifestyle. Not content with that, the brash envoy warned: "Your country will not last long! Having already lost the sense of order and discipline, how can you expect to survive?". The uncouth nature of the envoy's conduct and the unacceptable demand, led to the Korean refusal to pay any form of submission or respect to Hideyoshi. Naturally, Hideyoshi was furious at the failure and ordered that Yasuhiro and his entire family be killed. Sō Yoshishige was punished less severely, being replaced as daimyo of Tsushima by his adopted son Yoshitoshi, who Hideyoshi considered more trustworthy.

The incident not only led to a diplomatic failure but also resulted in a tragic loss of lives. The actions of Yasuhiro, the envoy sent by Yoshishige, were completely unacceptable and showed a lack of consideration for the diplomatic relations between Japan and Korea. The fact that Hideyoshi was furious and ordered the killing of Yasuhiro and his entire family, shows the severity of the situation and the importance placed on maintaining good relations with neighboring countries. It also highlights the brutal nature of the time period and the harsh consequences for those who did not meet the expectations of the ruling power.

THE KOREAN COURT'S UNDERESTIMATION

A Key Factor in the Invasion 1590

Over the next few years, more embassies were exchanged between Japan and Korea. However, in a crucial visit to Kyoto in 1590, Korean courtiers were unable to gather enough information about Hideyoshi's military strength, leading to an underestimation of the danger. This lack of knowledge also led to divisions among the Korean court factions, with members of the "Westerner" faction realizing the danger Japan posed but facing opposition from the "Easterner" group when trying to prepare for the invasion. This lack of unity and proper intelligence gathering would prove to be a critical factor in the Korean's ability to defend against the Japanese invasion.

HIDEYOSHI'S WAR MACHINE

The Invasion of Korea and its
Costly Consequences 1591

In Japan, a massive war machine was being prepared in the summer of 1591. The operation was led by Toyotomi Hideyoshi, who established a heavily fortified headquarters complex on the island of Kyushu. From there, he oversaw the levying of a massive army of 335,000 troops, with 158,000 of them crossing to Korea. The levies were raised by Japan's various daimyo lords, who, in a system known as gun'yaku, were obliged to supply a predetermined number of men according to the size and wealth of their fiefdom. Additional political factors, such as their personal standing with Hideyoshi, could also influence a daimyo's required contribution.

The 158,000-strong invasion force consisted of 82,200 men from Kyushu, which was closest to Korea, 57,000 from Honshu, and 19,600 from

Shikoku. The composition of this giant force must also be discussed. Contrary to popular belief, the majority of Hideyoshi's invading troops were not noble Samurai wielding katanas but rather humble ashigaru, peasant foot soldiers armed with swords, spears, and bows. Perhaps one-third of this army was armed with arquebuses, an early form of firearm introduced to Japan by the Portuguese.

Hideyoshi's plan was to conquer Asia in a domino effect. Once the Koreans were conquered, they would supply manpower and material for the push into China. The area around Beijing would then supply manpower for a push further into the Middle Kingdom, and so on. The idea was to expand his power and territory and gain control of the continent. However, this invasion would prove to be a costly and brutal war with a heavy toll on both sides.

The invading force would be ferried to Korea by 700 assorted ships which, along with their crews, were requisitioned from the various daimyo of the coastal provinces. These were mostly repurposed merchant or civilian vessels. Though Hideyoshi had a massive army at his disposal, in addition to high-quality military technology on land, naval power would prove a problem for him throughout the coming conflict. In contrast, the Koreans had just two advantages over the Japanese: their superior shipbuilding and cannon technology. However, these upsides were overshadowed by the fact that corruption in Korea was rampant, leaving military units neglected, untrained, and lazy. As a whole, the Joseon kingdom was not ready for the storm that was coming. However, one man within it, later to become Korea's most venerated war hero, Yi Sun-shin, was determined to be as prepared as possible. He spent a year diligently studying naval command, whipping his men into shape, and repairing infrastructure in his province of Cholla, which he recognized as a potential beachhead for the invasion.

THE BEGINNING OF THE JAPANESE INVASION OF KOREA

1592

In May 1592, three groups of the first wave of Japanese invaders were ready to sail. 18,700 troops under the command of Konishi Yukinaga and Sō Yoshitoshi set out for Busan without the protection of the warships that were meant to guard them. At first, the Korean commanders mistook the ships for a large trade mission, but soon realized it was an invasion. They had a chance to attack the undefended Japanese fleet with their superior warships, but due to lack of decisiveness and initiative, they failed to do so. The invasion had begun, and the Koreans were not fully prepared for it.

SIEGE OF BUSAN

1592

By May 1592, three contingents of the first wave of Japanese invaders were ready to sail. They set out for Busan with 18,700 troops under the command of Konishi Yukinaga and Sō Yoshitoshi without the protection of the warships that were meant to guard them. The Korean commanders initially mistook the ships for a large trade mission, but soon realized it was an invasion. They had a chance to attack the undefended Japanese fleet with their superior warships, but due to lack of decisiveness and initiative, they failed to do so. The invasion had begun, and the Koreans were not fully prepared for it. By nightfall on May 23rd, around 400 transports crowded the waters off Busan, resting in the harbour completely unopposed. After a final demand for an unopposed Japanese crossing to China was rejected, the troop landings began. At 4am on May 24th, 1592, 5,000 men under Yoshitoshi disembarked onto land, followed by another 7,000 under Yukinaga. Eventually, the entire first contingent had disembarked, and a Japanese army had landed on Korean soil without a single shot being fired. With Busan secured, the invading force pushed north along the middle of the peninsula, pillaging and plundering as they did. This led to panic among military leaders in surrounding provinces and attempts to mount opposition, but ultimately, the Koreans were unable to effectively resist the Japanese invasion.

In May 1592, three groups of the first wave of Japanese invaders were ready to sail. 18,700 troops under the command of Konishi Yukinaga and Sō Yoshitoshi set out for Busan without the protection of the warships that were meant to guard them. At first, the Korean commanders mistook the ships for a large trade mission, but soon realized it was an invasion. However, due to lack of decisiveness and initiative, the Koreans failed to attack the undefended Japanese fleet. The invasion had begun, and the Koreans were not fully prepared for it.

As the night fell on May 23rd, around 400 transports crowded the waters off Busan, resting in the harbor completely unopposed. After a final demand for an unopposed Japanese crossing to China was rejected, the troop landings began. At 4am on May 24th, 1592, 5,000 men under Yoshitoshi disembarked onto land, followed by another 7,000 under Yukinaga. Eventually, the entire first contingent had disembarked, and a Japanese army had landed on Korean soil without a single shot being fired. After two brief sieges, the main fortresses at Busan and its harbor fell, triggering panic among military leaders in surrounding provinces.

In yet another stunning act of military ineptitude, the incompetent Korean naval commanders scuttled their sizeable provincial fleets and destroyed their weaponry and provisions, retreating north as quickly as they could. With Busan secured, the proud Yukinaga refused to wait for reinforcements as instructed. Instead, he immediately pushed north along the middle of the peninsula on May 26th, marching at a blistering pace, likely wishing to monopolize the glory of seizing the capital for himself. This invading force first came to the deserted town of Yangsan, then went onto secure Miryang and Daegu on May 28th.

BATTLE OF CHUNGJU

1592

The Korean army, consisting of a mixture of cavalry troops, officers who had retreated from the south, and hastily raised levies from the north, could have potentially held the Choryong pass as per General Sin's original plan. However, upon learning that the pass had already been lost, Sin decided to engage in battle on an open field at Chungju. On June 6th, 1592, as the Japanese descended from the Choryong heights, Sin positioned his army on a flat stretch of land, surrounded by the hill called Tangumdae on one flank and the South Han river behind them. This was a strategic move, as placing troops in such a situation with no possibility of retreat was a tactic that had led to previous Chinese military victories. The Koreans hoped to use this tactic to defeat the Japanese, who they referred to as "robbers." However, as the Japanese army, led by daimyos Yukinaga and Kiyomasa, descended upon Chungju, tensions arose between the two leaders, with Kiyomasa seeking revenge on Yukinaga for stealing the glory of storming ahead. While Yukinaga advanced on the city from the southeast, the second contingent stayed behind, hoping for their rivals' defeat.

As the attacking troops approached the town, they spread out and faced off against General Sin's army in a wide arc. At 2 PM on June 6th, Yukinaga divided his army into three main units, with 10,000 soldiers under himself and Matsuura Shigenobu forming the vanguard, Sō Yoshitoshi and his 5,000 soldiers on the left flank, and 3,700 troops led by minor daimyos Arima Harunobu, Omura Yoshiaki, and Goto Sumiharu on the right. The front lines of the Japanese army were made up of arquebusiers, while ashigaru footmen armed with melee weapons stood behind them. As they advanced, the Japanese let out a roar of musket fire. Sin's forces, made up of amateur soldiers, were quickly overwhelmed by the flying arquebus balls and suffered heavy losses. The peasant soldiers began to flee, but Sin refused to retreat and led a charge of his crack cavalry towards the enemy line. However, the arquebusiers continued to rain down musket fire, breaking the charge before it could make contact. In a short amount of time, Sin's 8,000 strong army had been decimated and many survivors were hunted down by pursuing ashigaru. Sin ultimately took his own life by throwing himself into a spring while still wearing full armor.

The news of Sin Rip's defeat at Chungju caused panic in Seoul, and with no army to defend it, the Korean court decided to flee, despite the pleas of the populace. Konishi's decisive victory angered his rival commander Kato even more.
Some sources claim that Konishi was initially against the war, and, in a possible attempt to damage Hideyoshi's position, even warned the Korean court about the invasion, and was now moving quickly to erase any evidence of his betrayal. After almost coming to blows, the two daimyos took separate paths to Seoul. Konishi's route was easier, looping north and west where the Han River was not a decisive obstacle. At the same time, Kato took a shorter route directly north, but where the river was at its widest. After performing this river crossing with considerable ingenuity, Kato was shocked upon seeing the banners of his rival flying over the city's battlements. He had been beaten again by mere hours. Kuroda Nagamasa and his third contingent, as well as Ukita Hideie's 10,000 arrived on June 16th, 1592. The Korean capital itself was occupied with little bloodshed. Meanwhile, the Korean court had evacuated to Pyongyang. According to some sources, angered by their king's abandonment of them, the angry citizens burned many of the royal residences. Now that the capital

had been taken, the Japanese armies set out to consolidate their gains. The countryside
was pillaged largely without resistance. However, some Korean forces were still in the field.

BATTLE OF OKPO

1592

The Korean navy, led by Admiral Yi, set sail towards the east after meeting with Won at Dang'po. As they navigated around the edge of Koje Island and headed north, a scout ship approached them with news of a fleet of Japanese ships anchored at Ok-po port. This village, located in a large bay along the coast of Koje island, would become the site of the first naval battle of the war.

As the Korean naval forces entered the bay, Admiral Yi strategically positioned his smaller ships on the flanks while the larger and heavier warships formed a line in the center. He sent a message to his captains, instructing them to stand their ground and not to give way, but to "stand like mountain castles." With this, he ordered an advance.

The Japanese fleet, consisting of more than 50 transport ships, were caught off guard. Most of the ships were unmanned as the Japanese were looting and setting fire to the village. The smoke from the burning village obscured the view of the Korean ships, allowing them to approach unnoticed. The Japanese frantically tried to lift anchor and flee along the coast, but it was too late.

Admiral Yi's fleet attacked, engaging the Japanese at a distance and encircling them before unleashing a barrage of cannon fire and arrows to the beat of their admiral's war drum. The Japanese arquebusiers attempted to return fire, but the distance between the two fleets made it impossible for them to board the Korean ships. Gradually, the Japanese ships were destroyed one by one.

This battle, fought in the bay of Ok-po village, proved to be a pivotal moment in the war as it marked the first major victory for the Korean navy against the Japanese. Under the leadership and tactical brilliance of Admiral Yi, the Korean navy was able to emerge victorious and gain a significant advantage in the ongoing conflict.

The Korean navy, led by Admiral Yi Sun-shin, had a decisive victory against the Japanese navy in the battle near Ok-po. The Japanese fleet, consisting of 26 ships, were completely destroyed without a single loss for the Korean armada. The next day, another 13 Japanese ships were spotted near Jinhae, and once again, Yi's navy emerged victorious, destroying 11 out of those 13 ships without suffering any losses.

During these battles, Admiral Yi was known to take exotic trophies from the enemy ships, particularly their ornately decorated helmets. These were sent to King Seonjo as a symbol of the victories. The atrocities committed by the Japanese against the civilian population further fueled Yi's determination to defeat them.

After these victories, Yi retreated to Yeosu to reorganize his forces. The Japanese, realizing the Korean navy was still a formidable threat, sent another fleet to deal with Yi in early July. Being informed of this expedition, Yi set sail on July 8th with only 23 warships. He had replaced his smaller scout ships with something far more powerful and famous - the kobukson, also known as the turtle ship.

The turtle ship was a formidable vessel, measuring 28 meters in length, 9 meters in width, and 6 meters in height. It sat low in the water, allowing it to come under the Japanese castle ships and blast their hulls with cannon fire and archery. The sloping roof of planks bristling with iron spikes encased the vessel like the shell of a turtle, hence the name. Each turtle ship was equipped with around 15 advanced Korean cannons and a platform for archers.

BATTLE OF SACHION

1592

Admiral Yi Sun-shin, with his navy ready for battle, sailed to Sacheon where around 50 Japanese ships, including 12 warships, were anchored. The Japanese troops were stationed on the cliffs above the bay, and their commander, Wakizaka Yasuharu, had set up his command post there.

Yi knew that he couldn't risk closing in on the enemy with the added firepower from the land, but he also knew the Japanese's tendency to be arrogant. So, he devised a strategy of using a small force as bait, leading them to pursue the Koreans into the middle of the bay and then turning around and retreat, as though they were fleeing in terror.

Seeing this display of weakness, Yasuharu's men ran down from the heights and embarked on their ships to pursue the Korean navy. Admiral Yi, seeing the success of his lure, ordered an assault with the invulnerable turtle ships leading the charge. The turtle ships crashed into the middle of the enemy formation and unleashed a storm of cannon fire and arrows, causing massive losses among the Japanese vessels. The nimbler Korean vessels were also able to avoid Japanese boarding actions.

As the battle neared its end, and the enemy ships sank one by one, Yi was hit by a stray arquebus bullet in the shoulder. But, he remained stoic and after the battle was over, he supposedly withdrew a knife and dug the bullet out with it. When the battle was over, every ship that had pursued him was either burning on the sea or sunk.

The victories for the Korean navy led by Admiral Yi Sun-shin continued after the battle of Sacheon. First, at Dang'po, Yi defeated a 21-ship strong Japanese fleet, once again utilizing his turtle ships to break apart and wreak havoc within the enemy formation. Soon after, the Koreans advanced on a 26-strong anchored enemy armada at Danghangp'o, and all but one of the Japanese vessels were destroyed after Yi lured them into the open and smashed their battle line to pieces.

Despite the ongoing land war not going well for the Koreans, Yi made sure that the position of his kingdom was supreme on the sea. Back in Japan, Hideyoshi was furious at the continued resistance of this small Korean fleet and ordered his admirals

Wakizaka Yasuharu, Kato Yoshiaki, and Kuki Yoshitaka to stop their pointless inland plundering and annihilate Yi Sun-shin. The advancing Japanese armies needed supplies and reinforcements, but the Korean navy was preventing them. At the time, Yasuharu's 82 vessel fleet was the only one ready for the upcoming fight, and the proud daimyo chose to act alone in order to gain the glory from crushing Yi.

BATTLE OF HANSANDO

1592

The following morning, on August 15th, Admiral Yi Sun-shin deployed his fleet in a bay near the island of Hansando. Admiral Won suggested to attack Yasuharu's fleet head-on, but Yi refused. Instead of meeting the enemy in the narrows of Kyonnaerang, where the ships might collide with each other, he sent six panokson warships forward as bait for a trap. When these ships came within visual range of the enemy, they switched direction and fled, luring the Japanese fleet into a pursuit.

As they emerged into the open sea, the Korean fleet spread into a semicircular Crane's Wing formation, with light vessels on the flanks and heavier ships forming a sturdy center. When everything was in place, Yi ordered a charge. Immediately, the more nimble wings enveloped all of Yasuharu's vessels, darting in and out while showering the enemy with cannon fire and archery. At the same time, the heavier center, fronted by three turtle ships, smashed directly into the enemy formation.

Shooting from all sides, the turtle ships tore many Japanese ships apart with cannon fire, while the heavy panokson warships stayed at a distance and used their advantage in artillery to tear into the Japanese. In particular, metal-cased fire bombs were shot from mortars located on the decks of panokson craft. Only when the opposing ships were crippled did the admiral give the order to board and finish them off in melee combat.

After many hours of this drubbing, Yasuharu realized he was defeated and fled to a fast ship, barely managing to escape. Two of his relatives, Wakizaka Sabei and Watanabe Shichi'emon, were not so lucky, and were killed in the fighting. Of the 82 Japanese vessels that had sailed through Kyonnaerang that day, only 14 survived the Battle of Hansando. The two colleagues of Yasuharu whom he had left behind before the battle, Yoshitaka and Yoshiaki, were quickly informed of the disaster. They set sail immediately and reached Angolp'o, where they ran into the battered remnants of Yasuharu's forces. The victory at Hansando proved to be a significant blow to the Japanese navy, and further cemented Admiral Yi Sun-shin's reputation as a brilliant naval strategist and tactician.

BATTLE OF ANGOLPO

1592

The day following the Battle of Hansando, on August 16th, 1592, favourable winds prompted Admiral Yi Sun-shin to pursue his defeated enemy and arrived outside the Angolp'o harbour. He deployed his navy in the crane's wing formation once again, this time facing a total of 42 Japanese warships at anchor, protected by their own armaments, land fortifications on the nearby coast, and shallow waters in the bay itself.

Yi first attempted to lure the Japanese out with bait, as he had done many times before, but the Hansando experience had made his enemy wise to that tactic, and it garnered no response. Instead, the Korean admiral changed tactics and arranged for a continuous relay of ship squadrons to row into cannon range, unleash their destructive artillery volleys on the Japanese, and then withdraw to safety. This rolling bombardment was devastatingly successful. Almost all of the "pirates", as Yi called them, were killed, especially on the larger craft which had been the primary targets.

Seeing that a few ships had been left undamaged, Yi now called his vessels off. Many Japanese had escaped to the nearby shore and would probably wreak a terrible vengeance on Korean civilians if their means of escape was destroyed. Aiming to avoid unnecessary suffering among his people, the Joseon fleet withdrew to open water for the night. When they returned at dawn the following day, all Japanese survivors had fled, and the local inhabitants were unharmed. Yi still had not lost a single vessel in combat. The Battle of Angolp'o further solidified his reputation as a brilliant naval strategist and tactician, and it was one of his greatest victories of the war.

Admiral Yi Sun-shin was faced with a new challenge as troubling reports of ashigaru land armies advancing into Cholla reached him. He quickly withdrew to his base at Yeosu to strategize and plan his next move. Despite some Japanese prisoners managing to escape, Yi had already achieved great success in his naval campaign and was beginning to effectively strangle Japan's invasion of Korea. His reputation as a skilled and courageous leader was growing and his rise to become a national hero of Korea was just beginning.

While Yi was making a name for himself in the seas of the south, in the north of the country, the Japanese general Kato Kiyomasa was also seeking to gain glory and prestige. In early September, after capturing and sending two Korean princes down to Kyeong Seong with an armed escort of 1000 men, Kiyomasa prepared for a short incursion into Manchuria, where the semi-nomadic Jurchen tribes lived. The Japanese referred to these people as Orangai, derived from the Korean word 'oranke', which means barbarian.

This symbolic expedition against the barbarians across the Tumen river served a more practical purpose as well. Kiyomasa aimed to test his army against a possible future foe and collect valuable information on how the Jurchens fought. To aid him in this endeavor, he recruited Koreans from the Hamgyong province to act as his guides and vanguard. The locals had no love for the northern barbarians as they frequently raided their villages, so they were more than eager to offer their services to the Japanese.

With the addition of these Korean allies, Kiyomasa's army now totalled around 11000 men. He became the first Japanese general to cross into China, although he was unaware that he would also be the only one to do so at that time. His expedition was a significant event in the history of the invasion of Korea, and the actions of both Yi Sun-shin and Kato

Kiyomasa would be remembered as legendary feats of bravery and skill.

HAMGYONG CAMPAIGN

1592

The Japanese and their Korean allies soon came upon an Orangai castle and prepared to launch an assault at dawn. However, they soon realized that the castle was lightly defended and so, the Koreans advanced on the front of the fort while the Japanese troops went around the mountain to the rear of the fortress. Working in groups of 50 or 30, they managed to pull out the stones using crowbars and the wall collapsed. The Japanese entered the castle, and after some fierce arquebus volleys, they killed the small garrison and captured the Jurchen fortress.

Despite this success, Kiyomasa, who may have been aware of an incoming Jurchen counterattack, decided to pull back towards the Korean border and made camp for the night on a hill. The following morning, the Koreans headed back across the Tumen, leaving the Japanese to face an army of around 10,000 angry Jurchens. Although Kiyomasa's chronicler reports that for every Japanese dead, the Jurchens suffered 30 casualties, the attackers refused to give up and continued their ferocious assault.

The fight was so fierce that at one point Kiyomasa's standard bearer was killed next to him and the Japanese general had to hold it with his own hands. He also gave orders that the heads of the enemies were not to be collected as trophies, but only counted, as every samurai was needed for the fight. Despite the fierce resistance, the Japanese and their Korean allies were able to repel the Jurchen attack and return safely to their own territory.

Despite facing heavy resistance, Kato Kiyomasa's troops were able to successfully capture a Jurchen fortress and tally 8000 heads. However, the Jurchens continued to fight until an exceptionally heavy rain blew directly into their faces, forcing them to withdraw. Kiyomasa was pleased with the performance of his troops and the results of the short campaign. He crossed the Tumen river and continued eastwards towards the seas, capturing a series of Korean forts along the way.

Kiyomasa's expedition to Manchuria was the closest the Japanese came to invading China, their true objective. However, in order to amass a large enough force to invade the Middle Kingdom, they needed to dominate the sea around Korea. Admiral Yi, however, inflicted defeat upon defeat on the Japanese navy. One month after Kiyomasa's incursion over the Tumen river, Yi struck again, putting an end to Japanese ambitions of invading China.

Following the extraordinary success of the Hansando-Angolpo campaign, Admiral Yi returned to his base at Yosu in the Cholla Province. There, his fleet was reinforced with ships that had been hastily put into production upon the outbreak of the war. With 166 vessels under his command, 74 of which were large battleships, Yi Sun-sin planned to wash away the national disgrace and directly attack Busan.

BATTLE OF BUSAN

1592

Admiral Yi Sun-shin, joined by fellow commanders Yi Ok-ki and Won Kyun, reached the estuary of the Naktong river on the 4th of October and sent a scouting raft to investigate the situation. The raft returned with the report that 500 Japanese ships were anchored inside the city's harbor. Despite the daunting size of the Japanese fleet, the Korean admiral was emboldened by his previous victories and decided to attack the following day.

Facing a strong east wind and rough seas, the Korean fleet made its way towards Busan. In the waters just off the harbor, they encountered 24 Japanese ships organized in small groups. These ships were easily burned and destroyed, and the Koreans entered the harbor itself, where they witnessed the Japanese armada split into three large masses anchored near the shore.

The Japanese crews, realizing that there was no time to set sail and fight the enemy at sea, jumped overboard and headed for the fortifications on the heights above the shore, from where they would mount their defense. Just like in the battle of Sacheon, the Koreans approached as closely as they could and bombarded the unmanned Japanese ships with their cannons while also showering them with fire arrows.

The Japanese, well protected behind their fortifications, tried to prevent the destruction of their fleet by unleashing barrages of musket fire and arrows and making use of Korean cannons that had been captured in Busan and Dongnae, while others were frantically trying to repair their damaged ships. However, only the coming of night could stop the Koreans, who withdrew to the open seas after destroying 130 Japanese vessels. On the other hand, only five Koreans died during the battle and 25 were wounded, and Admiral Yi lost no ships.

Emboldened by his triumphant victory, Yi initially wanted to return to Busan the following morning and inflict further damage upon the Japanese, but he reconsidered his choice as the sinking of the entire fleet would leave the invaders trapped in Korea with no avenue of retreat. This strategy goes against Sun Tzu's Art of War, which advises against cutting off the enemy's retreat. The defeat at Busan and the loss of around a quarter of their fleet extinguished any lingering hopes the Japanese might have had of amassing an army in the north large enough to invade China. This victory by Admiral Yi Sun-shin was a turning point in the Imjin War, and it solidified his reputation as a national hero in Korea.

The victories Admiral Yi Sun-shin had won at sea had prevented the entry of his Japanese foes into the Yellow Sea, rendering them unable to reinforce and resupply their armies on land. Meanwhile, Korean ground forces behind the Japanese lines were doing the same. In the countryside and wilderness, guerilla armies began to form almost immediately, in reaction to the cruelty they and their countrymen experienced at the hands of the enemy. Resistance leaders such as Ko Kyong-myong, Cho Hon, and Kwak Chae-u set up ambushes to trap enemy troops and preyed on vulnerable Japanese supply barges that were using Korea's rivers for transport. These actions further hampered the logistics of Toyotomi Hideyoshi's conquering army in much the same way Admiral Yi was doing at sea.

Motivated partly by patriotism, and partly by a desire to raise the social status of their kin, an estimated 22,000 irregular fighters and 84,500 regular soldiers from the Yalu River in the north to the Naktong Delta in the south rejoined the fight as guerilla warriors in 1592, among them 8,000

Buddhist monks. In November of 1592, Korean guerilla forces contributed to the successful defense of Jinju, a battle which caused many Japanese casualties and humiliated the daimyo generals.

Most crucially, all of the chaos behind Hideyoshi

FIRST SIEGE OF JINJU

1592-1593

The siege of Jinju was a brutal and intense battle, with both sides determined to emerge victorious. The Japanese, with their superior numbers, were relentless in their attacks, but the Korean defenders were equally determined to hold their ground. The Korean artillery proved to be a significant advantage, as it inflicted heavy casualties on the Japanese attackers. The defenders also made use of their arquebuses, which were equal in quality to those of the Japanese, causing chaos among the invaders.

Despite the fierce resistance put up by the Koreans, the Japanese continued to press on. They constructed siege towers and used scaling ladders in an attempt to scale the walls, but the defenders were able to repel these attacks with their axes and stones. The Japanese also made use of their arquebusiers, who fired volleys over the walls, but the Koreans were able to counter this with their own artillery.

The siege lasted for three days, with the Koreans holding out against the relentless Japanese assault. On the final day, the Japanese decided to employ a clever strategy. They pretended to pack up their gear and prepare to leave, but in the early morning hours of November the 13th, they launched an all-out assault on the opposite side of the city along the northern and eastern gates. The Koreans rushed to defend, but during the battle, Kim Shimin was mortally wounded by a bullet in his left forehead, but this was kept from his men so they would not lose heart.

Despite this setback, the Koreans were able to repel the Japanese attack, thanks to the brave actions of their commander, Kim Shimin and the support of the guerilla force, the Righteous Army. The Japanese were forced to retreat, having suffered heavy casualties and failing to capture the castle. This was a significant victory for the Koreans, as it prevented the Japanese from advancing further into the Jeolla Province and provided a morale boost to the defenders.

The Korean garrison, which had been in a precarious position due to a lack of ammunition, was saved when a detachment of Korean troops arrived by boat up the Nam river, bringing with them much-needed supplies and encouraging the defenders to continue fighting. Despite the high number of casualties, the Japanese commanders were forced to halt their attack, as they feared a counterattack from the rear. This decision, much to the dismay of Hideyoshi, led to the abandonment of the siege and a retreat to Changwon under the cover of a sudden downpour. The Korean army, exhausted and low on supplies and ammunition, did not attempt to pursue the retreating Japanese.

However, the situation was about to become even more dire for the Japanese, as in late 1592, Ming China, which had long been a suzerain and protector of Korea, finally began its intervention in the war. Initially, a Chinese expeditionary force of 3,000 troops under the command of the reckless Zu Chengxun was ordered to take Pyongyang, but was ultimately destroyed when it became trapped and outnumbered inside the city. While this victory made the Japanese optimistic at first, the samurai commanders soon realized that the Chinese would be back soon, and in massive numbers.

Worried about this and the vulnerable state of Pyongyang, Konishi Yukinaga went south to Seoul in order to meet with his supreme commander, Ukita Hideie, to discuss these urgent matters. It turned out that Japanese anxieties were justified, for in January of 1593, after crushing the Ningxia revolt back home, the Chinese commander Li Rusong slowly led a large army of Ming troops into Korea, using scouts and spies to gather intelligence on Japanese positions as he advanced. After some minor skirmishes, Li Rusong's forces approached Pyongyang on February 5th.

SIEGE OF PYONGYANG

1593

The initial Japanese sortie from the gates of Pyongyang was crushed by a feigned retreat, but it was clear that recapturing the city would present a massive challenge. Pyongyang enjoyed a strong defensive position, flanked to the east by the Taedong River and northwest by the Pothong River. Moreover, it possessed some of Korea's most formidable walls, which had been continuously reinforced throughout the centuries, forming a crude, elongated triangle lying between the two rivers, within which were six gates. The entrances along the Taedong River were left lightly defended, with each of the four landward gates garrisoned by 2,000 Japanese soldiers apiece. Konishi Yukinaga and 2,000 elite bodyguard troops were deployed on Mount Moranbong, a 70-meter-high fortified vista from which a commanding view of surroundings could be had. Overall, roughly 15,000 men of the first contingent defended Pyongyang.

By the time he arrived at Pyongyang, Li Rusong's 43,000 strong Imperial army had been further swollen by many thousands of Koreans and 5,000 warrior monks. He set up his own headquarters on high ground west of the Pothong River, personally commanding 9,000 troops. Around the city, the general distributed various detachments under his subordinates to assault the various gates. 10,000 soldiers under Zhang Shijue were set up opposite the Chilsong gate, 11,000 under Yang Yuan formed up facing the Pothong gate, and a further 10,000 under Li Rubo prepared to assault the Hangu gate. Finally, 9,000 Koreans under their native commanders Yi Il and Kim Ungso were ordered to the Changyong gate. The Chinese cannons, capable of firing large stones over two kilometers, were distributed evenly around the siege lines under heavy guard.

After an attempt to translate Konishi Yukinaga failed, the assault began. Spearheading the assault were 3,000 warrior monks, capable warriors under the command of Hyujong, a master monk. On the morning of February 6th 1593, these brave religious warriors advanced up the northern slope of Mount Moranbong, attempting to scale the hill walls. In the face of withering arquebus fire from the Japanese on the fortifications, they suffered hundreds of casualties, but persevered nonetheless. As the defenders began to tire in the late afternoon, the monks were joined by a Chinese unit under

We Weizhong, whose troops began to scale Mount Moranbong from the west. This contingent began to breach the area, streaming onto the mountain behind Yukinaga's lines. All of a sudden, Yukinaga was surrounded, and there was a danger he would be killed. At that moment, Sō Yoshitomo: a compatriot of Yukinaga, led a counterattack from the main city and broke the Chinese encirclement on Mount Moranbong, allowing the remnants of Yukinaga's 2,000 strong guard to retreat. That evening, the Japanese abandoned the mountain, instead taking up positions in their recently constructed citadel, a construction of primitive earthworks.

The next morning, Li Rusong ordered a general assault on Pyongyang with all forces engaged. As the first blast of cannon fire sounded, the general advanced at the head of his troops, only to be met with a storm of Japanese arquebus fire, rocks, arrows and boiling water. Aiming to blunt this dogged resistance, Ming cannons continuously battered the walls and gates of Pyongyang, aiming to soften them up. At the same time, incendiary bombs and fire arrows were loosed into the city itself, causing chaos, setting fire to buildings and even the forest outside of the city. Under the hail of projectiles, Chinese and Jose

Now under intense pressure, the defensive ring along the walls of Pyongyang fell apart, resulting in a Japanese withdrawal to the inner citadel. This hastily constructed fortification was apparently built with holes in its side for arquebusiers to fire through, which caused it to look like a beehive. The sophisticated Chinese officers, looking with scorn at the 'primitive' and 'barbarian' citadel, immediately ordered an assault in massed ranks. This proved to be a dreadful mistake. Japanese troops fired volley after volley of arquebus shots into the tightly packed Ming and Korean soldiers, causing massive casualties and breaking the assault's momentum. When Yukinaga saw some enemies retreating from the city altogether, he led a sortie from the citadel in an attempt to break the siege, but was methodically driven back by concentrated Chinese cannon fire.

As daylight waned, the Japanese were still in control of the inner fortress, but were badly bloodied. Li Rusong decided to pull his men back for the night so that they could rest. Meanwhile, inside the citadel, Yukinaga held a war council. It was quickly decided their position was untenable and the Japanese decided to retreat. Under the cover of darkness, the entire remaining garrison quietly withdrew through the Changyong gate and across the frozen Taedong River. According to samurai Yoshino Jingoza'emon, who was present during the retreat, wounded men were routinely abandoned, while those exhausted men simply crawled along the road. Yukinaga's men hoped to rest at a communication fort at Pungsan, but it had been abandoned by its commander, who assumed Yukinaga had already been annihilated.

This Ming-dominated victory at Pyongyang was a change in momentum. While at the start of the war the Japanese had seemed unstoppable, it was now Li Rusong's army that advanced, and the Japanese who were in a headlong retreat. Nevertheless, the Japanese sixth contingent under Kobayakawa Takakage managed to lure Li into a trap, defeating his army at the battle of Byeokjegwan. This would prove to be one of the biggest pitched battles of the invasion, and one which the Chinese general only narrowly escaped before withdrawing his army north to recover.

Having heard of the Ming victories in the north and at Pyongyang, a gifted Korean general known as Gwon Yul marched 2,300 troops to garrison the fortress of Haengju, situated on a hill 13 kilometers north of Seoul. The fortress was strategically important, as it controlled the road leading to the capital city of Hanyang (present-day Seoul) and it was also an important supply hub for the Japanese army. Gwon Yul, with his small but skilled army, held off multiple Japanese attacks and prevented them from advancing further north, buying precious time for the Ming army to regroup and launch counterattacks. This was a significant turning point in the war as it hindered the Japanese advance and prevented them from capturing the capital city.

SIEGE OF HAENGJU

1593

The delay caused by Li Rusong's tactical defeat in the war between Japan and China in 1593 gave the Japanese some breathing room and allowed Ukita Hideie to march straight at Haengju with 30,000 soldiers, among whom were the reconstituted forces of Yukinaga who had regrouped after fleeing Pyongyang. They fully expected to crush the tiny and bothersome force without any issue. However, the ensuing battle would not go the way the Japanese were expecting it to.

At 6am on the 14th of March 1593, Ukita's army encircled Haengju and marched up the slopes leading up to it from all directions. Unbeknownst to the Japanese, however, the Koreans were waiting and ready for them. Dug in behind formidable entrenchments, Gwon Yul's forces sent a barrage of bowfire, arquebus shots, delayed-action mortar bombs, rocks and even tree trunks down on the attackers. Most infamous were the Korean hwacha: medieval rocket launchers capable of loading up to 100 steel tipped rockets. Despite this rabidly fearsome defense, Japan's numerical superiority paid off, and the Koreans were forced back to the second defensive line, but their artillery caused devastating casualties upon the massed Japanese waves. Nine attacks were made in total, and all nine attacks were repelled. Overall, some sources claim up to 10,000 attackers ended up dead or wounded. Outnumbered by more than 10 to 1, Gwon Yul had gained victory.

This remarkable triumph prompted the Chinese commander, Li Rusong, to once again move south. Having been despondent after his prior defeat against the Japanese, his huge Ming army now advanced south once again. In Seoul, the situation was horrible for the Japanese soldiery. Frostbite, starvation and disease had worn down the expeditionary army to around 53,000 total troops from its original 150,000, and it was clear that operations would need to cease for the time being. The remaining armies of Japan decided on a southward retreat to their coastal fortress at Busan, and as a result, the Chinese army liberated Seoul on May 19th.

After this, logistical constraints and a cautious approach meant that the war ground down into a stalemate, with neither side making any decisive movements. Diplomacy also took place during this unenforced truce, and Li Rusong sent envoys to meet with the daimyo generals in Busan, discussing topics such as troop withdrawal from the provinces and assigning blame for the war. Nevertheless, this was not an indication that Japan was militarily spent, and the generals now began to prepare for a punitive destruction of Jinju. Hideyoshi's forces had failed to take the strongly fortified city in 1592, much to their humiliation and dishonor, and they would now avenge that loss. So, despite negotiating with the Ming Chinese at the same time, Hideyoshi sent the order to wipe Jinju off the map. Having heard of the Japanese plans, the Koreans had managed to assemble around 4,000 troops in the city, ready to defend it to the death.

The Battle of Haengju, where Gwon Yul's outnumbered army defeated the Japanese army and the subsequent retreat of the Japanese army to their coastal fortress at Busan, was a turning point in the war between Japan and China in 1593. The victory at Haengju had an immediate impact on the morale of the Chinese army, who were now determined to push forward and liberate Seoul. The defeat also forced Japan to rethink their strategy and prepare for a new battle in Jinju. The war would continue for several more years, but the tide had clearly turned in favor of China

SECOND SIEGE OF JINJU

1593

On the twentieth of July 1593, splendid commander Ukita Hideie arrived out of doors the metropolis with an navy

90,000 guys strong, swollen through recent reinforcements from the homeland. To the western fringe of the metropolis, Konishi Yukinaga commanded 26,000 guys, whilst his rival Kato Kiyomasa led

25,000 to the north. On the japanese flank of Jinju became Ukita Hideie himself, with 17,000 troops under

his leadership. Behind those attack forces became a ring of Japanese troops dealing with outward, to guard

in opposition to any feasible Ming attack at the siege lines. Furthermore, the besieging navy placed

contingents at the hills close to the metropolis in order to repel any reinforcements that got here to relieve Jinju. To the northwest Kobayakawa Takakage, the victor of Byeokjegwan, held authority over 8,700

troops, whilst Mori Hidemoto had been stationed to the northeast with 13,000. Finally, Kikkawa Hiroie had

numerous thousand extra throughout the Nam river, to easy up any problem to the metropolis's south.

Throughout July 21st, the Japanese laboured to drain the newly constructed moat out of doors the metropolis.

In this, they determined restricted success, as outer sections of the dykes had been destroyed, and the channel became full of rocks, earth and brushwood. This set the level for a fashionable assault

at the landward facet of the metropolis the subsequent day. Using scaling ladders to hurricane the partitions, Japanese

troops fought fiercely and nearly penetrated the metropolis's defenses, however smart Korean use of artillery and hearthplace arrows drove them again. As the twenty third dawned, huge and static siege towers had been

built on the way to facilitate observation and arquebus hearthplace into the metropolis. However, this became now no longer successful, as detrimental Korean cannon hearthplace shot the towers to portions one through one.

Things regarded to be searching higher for the defenders whilst a neighborhood navy marched towards Jinju from the east in an try to relieve it. However,

those reinforcements had been quick driven away through Hidemoto's northeast rearguard. On July 25th,

Hideie despatched a message into the castle, calling on Gim Cheonil, the garrison commander, to give up.

The splendid commander obtained no reply. Japanese forces attempted once more at the 26th.

This time a chain of 'tortoise shell wagons' with boarded roofs had been built, providing

safety for advancing troops whilst sappers mined basis stones from the ramparts. It

made a few progress, however this attack became driven again whilst bundles of combustibles dropped off

the partitions had been set alight, burning the protective shells. Nevertheless, it became turning into clean that

the garrison became going for walks out of factors to throw at Hideie's navy. Undaunted through the preceding failure,

Kato Kiyomasa ordered that new tortoise wagons had been to be readied, and this time fireproofed through protecting them with ox hide. On the twenty seventh a brand new assault commenced which targeted on

the cornerstones of the northeastern section of the wall. During the day, a heavy rainstorm broke out which undermined the foundations, sooner or later

collapsing this forced section.
Taking gain of the breach, Japanese troops commenced to hurricane the metropolis thru the gap. Korean
resistance collapsed nearly straight away after this. Gim Cheonil, staring at activities from a tower withinside the centre of Jinju, determined to devote suicide in place of give up to the enemy.

The siege of Jinju by the Japanese army, led by Kikkawa Motoharu, was a devastating and brutal event that resulted in a massacre of both civilians and soldiers. The exact number of casualties remains uncertain, with some records indicating that as many as 20,000 people were killed, while others suggest the death toll could have been as high as 60,000. The Nam River, which flowed through the city, was said to have turned red with blood as a result of the carnage, and the banks of the river were said to be littered with headless corpses.

Despite the brutal nature of this Japanese victory, it ultimately had little impact on the overall course of the war. The Japanese were soon forced to retreat back to the chain of coastal fortresses they controlled in the south, known as wajo. Negotiations began, a ceasefire was imposed, and a Ming emissary was sent to Japan to discuss terms with Toyotomi Hideyoshi. Gradually, the daimyo and their men began to return to their homeland.

To the north, the Chinese also withdrew their expeditionary force, and though peace talks would continue for years after this, the first invasion of Korea was essentially over. King Seonjo arrived back in the Joseon capital of Seoul on October 24th, 1593, after an exile of more than a year. Though the majority of his country had been reclaimed, it was completely drained of resources and its population was in the grips of terrible famine. Royal treasuries were empty, many productive settlements had been destroyed, and much economic devastation had been caused by the war.

The rebuilding effort was headed by newly appointed Prime Minister Ryu Seong-ryong, who prioritized national defense. All over the nation, and especially in the Japanese-occupied south, the Joseon government began to construct impregnable mountain fortresses, situated to take advantage of the terrain. Furthermore, modernization reforms in the Joseon military were undertaken from late 1593 onwards. Unit organization was tuned and adjusted, and new weapons such as modern firearms and more advanced battle tactics were adopted. Reconstruction throughout the following years gradually brought normalcy back to Korean life, but this also came with the dangers that had plagued King Seonjo's government before the war, as factional court politics now re-emerged. The labyrinthine rivalry between westerner and easterner factions reignited with greater intensity than before, as the country struggled to recover from the devastating effects of the war.

INFIGHTING AND INTRIGUE

1593-1596

The Prime Minister, who was a highly respected and influential member of the eastern faction, was deemed too powerful and well-protected for his enemies to directly target. Instead, they chose to focus their efforts on a more vulnerable individual who was closely associated with the Prime Minister. This individual was none other than Admiral Yi Sun-shin, who had been a childhood friend of Ryu Seong-ryong, and had recently been promoted to the position of commander of the Korean navy in the south. The westerners, who sought to discredit and undermine the reputation of Admiral Yi, had a secret weapon in their arsenal: Won Gyun, who was an underling of Yi and had previously served as his subordinate. During the first Japanese invasion, Won Gyun had been known to be cunning and deceitful, constantly sending unfavourable reports about Yi to his superiors, based on nothing but lies and fabrications. This factional infighting and internal strife among the Korean leaders was a cause for concern, especially since, as these events were unfolding, diplomatic failures between Japan and China had provoked Toyotomi Hideyoshi into preparing a second invasion of Korea.

THE FALL OF ADMIRAL YI SUN-SHIN

1597

In comparison to the grand continental conquest envisioned in the prior assault, this second attack was to be a simple grab for Korea's southern half. One of the most important lessons learned by the daimyo was just how critical of a threat the Korean navy was. So, the Japanese commanders aimed to achieve supremacy at sea by two means: assembling a far stronger fleet than the one before, and weakening the enemy fleet by neutralizing its prodigious commander: Admiral Yi. To that end, Japanese forces began heavily reinforcing their armies in Korea. In addition to the roughly 20,000 remaining garrison troops in the coastal wajo fortresses, 121,000 more soldiers were to be mobilized. Under the supreme authority of the fifteen-year-old Kobayakawa Hideaki, Japanese soldiers ever so slowly began returning to enemy soil in March of 1597.

After they did, Hideyoshi's forces did not launch an instant assault, but instead stalled for months on end waiting for harvest season. By plundering local farmers during this plentiful time of year, the Japanese forces could live off the land more easily, relatively unaided by vulnerable supply lines. Moreover, Hideyoshi's plan was to march through the southwest province of Cholla - known as the breadbasket of Korea. Before the land invasion even began, events at sea were to prove utterly disastrous for the defenders as Japanese intrigue bore fruit. Konishi Yukinaga sent a spy named Yojiro to inform the Korean high command that he was eager to extinguish his rival, Kato Kiyomasa, for good. To this end, he provided a precise location as to where the lethal Korean navy could easily ambush the hated commander at sea. The gullible Joseon court believed him, and sent Yi Sun-shin the order to prepare the attack.

However, the Japanese had played a cunning game and the ambush was a trap set by Kato Kiyomasa himself, who was aware of the plan and had set the location to lure the Korean navy into a trap. This resulted in the defeat of the Korean navy and the capture of Admiral Yi Sun-shin, which would prove to be a significant blow to the defense of Korea. The Japanese had succeeded in neutralizing the threat posed by the Korean navy, which would prove to be a crucial factor in the outcome of the second invasion of Korea. The events that transpired at sea before the land invasion even began, were a clear indication of the level of cunning and deceit employed by the Japanese commanders in their efforts to conquer Korea.

Upon receiving this order, Admiral Yi Sun-shin was immediately suspicious. He did not trust the Japanese-given information and thought that this plan sounded far too easy. The admiral refused to obey the order and decided to investigate the situation further. In response, officials were dispatched to depose and arrest the heroic naval commander, replacing him with none other than the wily intriguer himself, Won Gyun, who immediately began proving himself totally incompetent.

Admiral Yi Sun-shin avoided execution by the skin of his teeth, but was demoted to the status of a common soldier. This Japanese ploy had worked wonders, and it seemed the dangerous admiral Yi was neutralized forever. Soon after this, Yojiro once again informed the Joseon court of a location where they could easily ambush another Japanese fleet. However, this time, Admiral Yi was not present to advise caution and the Korean fleet was led by the incompetent Won Gyun.

On the 17th of August, Admiral Won Kyun, heavily

pressed by his superior, Kwon Yul, gathered the entire Korean fleet, slightly over 200 ships and set sail eastwards towards Busan. However, the Japanese were well informed of the movements of the Korean fleet through their network of spies on the hills that overlooked Hansando. They had received accurate information about the size, composition and movements of the Korean fleet, which allowed them to prepare a devastating counter-attack.

This proved to be a fatal mistake for the Koreans as the Japanese fleet was far superior in both numbers and capabilities, and the Korean fleet was decimated in the ensuing battle. This devastating defeat was a direct result of the Japanese's intricate plot to neutralize Admiral Yi, the most capable and experienced commander of the Korean navy, through deceit and trickery. The absence of Admiral Yi's leadership and strategic insight proved to be a crucial factor in the outcome of the battle and the fate of the Korean defense.

BATTLE OF CHICHEOLLYYANG

1597

Three days later, as the Korean ships neared Cholyongdo, they encountered the main Japanese fleet, which numbered between 500 to 1000 ships strong, already arrayed in a vast line. The battle had not even begun and the Koreans were already at a disadvantage, exhausted from the long day at sea and with little faith in their leader's abilities. Despite the odds being heavily stacked against him, Won Kyun ordered a general attack. The Japanese feigned a retreat with the Koreans pursuing them, but afterwards they turned and drove them back. After repeatedly moving back and forth, the Japanese decided to finally attack with all their might. In this charge, they managed to destroy 30 Korean vessels, and because of this, the rest of the terrified Korean fleet soon routed.

Despite this, the disaster was not yet over. Some of the ships, having reached Kadok island, decided to make a quick stop to refresh their supplies in water. The island was garrisoned by a large Japanese force, and soon they were met with 3000 soldiers under Shimazu Yoshihiro's banner, who killed around 400 Koreans and destroyed several more vessels. Whatever remained from the Korean fleet continued to retreat until they reached Chilcheollyang, a narrow strait between Koje and Chilchon island and stayed there for a week.

The defeat at Busan and the reprimand he received from Kwon Yul severely crippled Won's morale, who retired to his flagship and refused to talk to anyone, thus leaving the fleet headless. The Japanese, after having experienced defeat at the hands of Yi Sunshin time and again, were now eager to exploit this naval success to its fullest, and so they pursued the Korean fleet westwards. Unaware of the incoming Japanese attack, Won Kyun did little to plan a defense or boost his men's morale. Finally, a few hours after midnight, on August 28th, the Japanese fleet numbering almost 500 ships and under the light of a full moon reached Chilcheollyang. Three guns signaled the attack and the Japanese fell upon their prey with arrows and gun fire.

The Korean fleet was caught off guard and had no chance to defend themselves, as they were still reeling from the defeat at Busan and the lack of leadership from Won Kyun.

Any Korean ships which weren't set on fire were boarded, with their crews cut down. The Koreans who were unaccustomed to night warfare, and thoroughly demoralized, offered little resistance. Some of them tried to escape by landing on the nearby Koje island, but as it had been on Kadok island, they were met with a Japanese ambush party who mowed them down. Admiral Won also met his fate as he was trying to escape to the mainland. By dawn, all but 13 ships would be lost.

These 13 ships were commanded by Bae Sol, who, having realized that the straight was a dangerous spot, had moved them farther away. These 13 ships would later become the saviors of Korea at Myeongdong. News of the disaster reached Seoul soon after it occurred, and the king swiftly made the only decision he could: reinstating the disgraced Yi Sun-Shin as supreme naval commander. With the seas around Korea now swept clean of enemy ships, the two Japanese ground thrusts began on September 11th, comprising Ukita Hideie's 49,600 strong Left Army and Mori Hidetomo's 65,300 strong Right Army.

This was to be a brutal and pitiless invasion, undertaken with a degree of savagery unseen in 1592. Hideyoshi's orders now were to "Mow down everyone universally, without discriminating between young and old, men and women, clergy and laity". With this in mind, the advance began. The Army of the Left marched through Jeolla province and reached the fortified town of Namwon on the 23rd of September 1597.

The town of Namwon was a strategically important location, as it sat at the confluence of the Namwon and Jeonnam Rivers, and was a key transportation hub for the region.

SIEGE OF NAMWON

1592

The city of Namwon was situated on a flat plain, with its only natural defense being a river flowing to the south that acted as a distant moat. The walls of the city were not particularly tall, standing at approximately 4 meters in height, but they were plastered with shell-lime and tiny fragments of seashells, which caused them to glitter in the sun and created an impressive spectacle. In order to provide additional defense, bastions were formed between each gate and wall corner, allowing for flanking fire onto the gates.

In the area around the city, there was an alternative defensive position just to the north, the mountain fortress of Kyoryong. This fortress was more naturally suited to withstand an attack by the Japanese, as the enemy would have had to fight an uphill battle through a heavily forested area. Because of this, the Korean garrison of the Namwon had advocated for abandoning the city and moving to Kyoryong. However, the Ming general Yang Yuan, who perhaps had more confidence in defending a Chinese-style fortification, overruled them and chose to stay in Namwon. This decision would later prove to be fatal.

To his credit, Yang Yuan did not sit idly waiting for the arrival of the Japanese, but worked to strengthen the city's defenses. Another three meters were added to the wall's height, and cannons were placed on the main gatehouses. The defenders also dug a ditch that was 6 meters deep, enclosed by a wooden palisade, with spiked tree trunks laid at the bottom to slow down the Japanese assault. Furthermore, a fortified water reservoir was built outside the walls to prepare the city for a lengthy siege, and fences were constructed on the fields. Finally, as the defenses were almost complete, Yang Yuan ordered the destruction of Kyoryong to prevent the Japanese from using it.

When the Japanese army arrived, they immediately besieged the city from all sides, leaving no escape routes for the 12,000 people now trapped inside, half of whom were civilians. Hideie was in command of the southern sector, while Konishi Yukinaga commanded the west, Kurushima Michifusa and Kato Yoshiaka's troops covered the northern side, and 11 other generals secured the eastern approach. Seeing that the invaders were busy with constructing their own defenses, the besieged garrison decided to sally out, but were met with rapid volleys of arquebus fire and were forced to retreat into the city.

The next day, the Japanese began filling the city's defensive ditch with earth and straw, all the while under heavy cannon, musket, and arrow fire from the walls. When this was done, many of their own arquebusiers crossed over and, by taking cover in the burnt houses and the fences outside the walls, began to harass the defenders. That following evening, the Japanese sent a delegation asking for the defenders to surrender, but this offer, like all other occasions, was rejected. As a result, the Japanese resumed their offense with increased fervor, which continued well into the night despite heavy rain.

The solution to the stalemate came for the besiegers in the form of a clever stratagem. Witnessing the still-green rice stalks on the nearby fields, they cut them, then tied them together in large bundles. When darkness began to fall, the Japanese unleashed a heavy cannon barrage accompanied by arquebus fire that lasted for 2 hours and forced the defenders to keep their heads down. Under the cover of night and the suppressive volleys of their guns, they quietly built a ramp out of the rice stalks. As the barrage stopped, the Japanese troops assaulted the walls, with the samurai Matsuura Shigenobu reportedly leading the way.

Keinen, a priest who was accompanying the army as a physician, was so shocked by what he witnessed during the second invasion of Japan, that he later wrote in his poems: "Whoever sees this, Out of all his days, Today has become the rest of his life." The final act of barbarism committed by the Japanese during this invasion was that they cut off the noses of 3,726 dead, salted them, and then shipped them back to Japan as proof to Hideyoshi that they had fought and defeated their opponents. Overall, in this second invasion, momentum had thus far been solely on Japan's side.

However, the tide would begin to turn when a small number of Ming reinforcements, led by General Yang Hao, managed to ambush and defeat Japanese forces at Jiksan. This prevented any further incursions toward Seoul, and marked the furthest Japan would encroach into Korean territory. The daunting prospect of more gigantic Chinese armies joining the Koreans, and a forthcoming winter, meant that turning back south was the only realistic choice for the Japanese.

With the invasion on land stalling in late 1597, it is here that Yi Sun-shin is thrust back into the limelight. After being reinstated as naval commander in the south, the Admiral had only thirteen ships to work with. Nevertheless, his mere presence cheered up the local population, who often greeted him as a savior. "Our admiral has come again, now we can be safe!" shouted one local peasant. However great his bravery or ability, what could Admiral Yi do with only thirteen ships against hundreds?

Firstly, he set about reasserting discipline and order. Guards were posted to protect armories and storehouses, cowardly officials were reprimanded and sent back to work, officers and enlisted men were flogged for dereliction, and civilians were punished for any offense. Through these harsh means, Yi restored to himself what traditional Chinese military doctrine dubbed 'awesomeness': the mix of fear and respect a leader needed to command effectively.

Reaching his small fleet at Hoeryongpo, he immediately retrofitted all vessels to serve as makeshift turtle-ships, with sturdy timber sides and spiked roofs to protect the crews. When this was done, Yi sailed kilometers west to Oranpo, which had a more open harbour. He knew that his fleet was no match for the Japanese navy, but he believed that by using the geography of the coast and his knowledge of the sea, he could defeat the Japanese in a series of small engagements. His strategy was to wear down the enemy's morale and supplies, while conserving his own, and then deliver the final blow when the opportunity presented itself.

BATTLE OF MYEONGNYANG

1597

It was about this time that Yi Sun-shin, the naval commander, received intelligence that the main Japanese war fleet was after him, so he retreated to the island of Chindo, further to the west. A 13-strong scout fleet tried to destroy Yi on the 17th of October, but was fought off without much difficulty. In the days after this minor skirmish, the main Japanese fleet arrived at Oranpo and began building up its strength. As they did, Yi spent his time carefully observing the properties of surrounding bodies of water, noting the current speed, direction, and time of the tide.

Of particular interest to the admiral was the narrow Myeongnyang Channel, a stretch of water only 250 meters wide at its narrowest point. The current was also among the fastest in all Korea, moving at a faster speed than Japanese ships could travel. This was a perfect place to make a final stand. On

October 24th, Yi received further intelligence that a 200-ship-strong Japanese fleet was closing in on his position. In response, he pulled his fleet through the Myeongnyang strait the next day, anchoring his ships in the open water just outside it. Beyond Yi's 13 combat vessels was a long line of fishing boats packed with refugees. By arranging these vessels in a mock battle line, the admiral hoped that the Japanese would assume his own squadron was merely the vanguard of a larger force. That night, with everything set as he wanted, Yi summoned his commanders to an audience, telling them that "He who seeks death shall live! He who seeks his life shall die!".

At dawn, the next day, the main Japanese armada of two to three hundred vessels approached the southern end of the Myeongnyang Strait. As Yi had predicted, this huge mass of ships was unable to pass through the narrow channel of Myeongnyang in one group, and thus began to split into separate squadrons. Everything was going according to Yi's plan. It was only when the first enemy ships began to emerge into the open water that Yi ordered the attack. The Japanese fleet had not realized the Koreans were there, but were finally notified by the cannons and fire arrows that began to attack them.

However, as the admiral's flagship blasted the stunned enemy warships, the other ships in his fleet began to lag behind, witnessing the extraordinary odds they faced. But, threats of punishment and Yi's dogged determination motivated his captains to catch up and fight. At this point, the meager 13-ship Korean fleet was completely enveloped by at least 130 Japanese vessels. Nevertheless, Yi's ships were able to move faster and more nimbly in the narrow channel, and the Japanese ships were unable to maneuver effectively in the fast-moving currents.

It was during this pivotal moment in the war that Yi Sun-shin, the renowned naval commander, received intelligence that the main Japanese war fleet was on the hunt for him. In light of this information, he retreated to the island of Chindo, located further to the west. On the 17th of October, a scout fleet of 13 ships attempted to destroy Yi and his fleet, but their efforts were met with little success and were easily fought off.

In the days that followed this minor skirmish, the main Japanese fleet arrived at Oranpo and began to build up their strength. As they did so, Yi spent his time carefully observing the properties of the surrounding bodies of water, taking note of the current speed, direction, and time of the tide. Of particular interest to the admiral was the narrow Myeongnyang Channel, a stretch of water that was only 250 meters wide at its narrowest point. The current in this channel was also among the fastest in all of Korea, moving at a speed that Japanese ships could not match. This, Yi recognized, was the perfect place to make a final stand.

On October 24th, Yi received further intelligence that a fleet of 200 Japanese ships was closing in on his position. In response, he pulled his fleet through the Myeongnyang strait the following day, anchoring his ships in the open water just outside it. Beyond Yi's 13 combat vessels was a long line of fishing boats, each packed with refugees. By arranging these vessels in a mock battle line, the admiral hoped that the Japanese would assume his own squadron was merely the vanguard of a larger force.

That night, with everything set as he wanted, Yi summoned his commanders to an audience and told them, "He who seeks death shall live! He who seeks his life shall die!". At dawn the next day, the main Japanese armada of two to three hundred vessels approached the southern end of the Myeongnyang Strait. As Yi had predicted, this huge mass of ships was unable to pass through the narrow channel of Myeongnyang in one group, and thus began to split into separate squadrons. Everything was going according to Yi's plan. It was only when the first enemy ships began to emerge into the open water that Yi ordered the attack. The Japanese fleet had not realized the Koreans were there, but were finally notified by the cannons and fire arrows that began to attack them.

However, as the admiral's flagship blasted the stunned enemy warships, the other ships in his fleet began to lag behind, witnessing the extraordinary odds they faced. But, through threats of punishment and Yi's dogged determination, his captains were motivated to catch up and fight. At this point, the meager 13-ship Korean fleet was completely enveloped by at least 130 Japanese vessels. Nevertheless, Yi's ships were able to move faster and more nimbly in the narrow channel, and the Japanese ships were unable to maneuver effectively in the fast-moving currents, allowing for the tide of the battle to turn in favor of the Korean fleet.

END OF JAPAN'S CONQUEST OF KOREA

1598

By March of 1598, the Korean naval forces, under the leadership of Admiral Yi Sun-shin, had made significant progress in their efforts to defend their country against the invading Japanese armies. A total of 61 warships were ready for combat and a further 39 were under construction at the many shipyards scattered throughout the country. These successes at sea were accompanied by further victories on land, as Ming reinforcements had arrived and, joining forces with the Korean troops, were able to pin the land armies of Toyotomi Hideyoshi in their chain of coastal fortresses.

Then, on September 18th 1598, Toyotomi Hideyoshi, the leader of the Japanese invasion, passed away at the age of 62. This was the final nail in the coffin of Japan's attempted conquest of Korea.

One of the great Kwampaku's final orders was for the conflict to be brought to an end and for all soldiers to return home. Both Hideyoshi's son, Hideyori, and other powerful daimyo such as Tokugawa Ieyasu were also eager to see the costly war stopped. Additionally, the Ming were receptive to the idea of allowing Konishi Yukinaga and the other wajo garrisons to escape back to their homeland unharmed. However, the vengeful Koreans were not willing to accept this and sought to continue their efforts to drive the Japanese out of their country.

BATTLE OF NORYANG

1598

It was about this time that Admiral Yi Sun-shin received intelligence that the main Japanese war fleet was after him, so he retreated to the island of Chindo, further to the west. A 13-strong scout fleet tried to destroy Yi on the 17th of October, but was fought off without much difficulty. In the days after this minor skirmish, the main Japanese fleet arrived at Oranpo and began building up its strength. As they did, Yi spent his time carefully observing the properties of surrounding bodies of water, noting the current speed, direction, and time of the tide. Of particular interest to the admiral was the narrow Myeongnyang Channel, a stretch of water only 250 meters wide at its narrowest point. The current was also among the fastest in all Korea, moving at a faster speed than Japanese ships could travel. This was a perfect place to make a final stand.

On October 24th, Yi received further intelligence

that a 200-ship-strong Japanese fleet was closing in on his position. In response, he pulled his fleet through the Myeongnyang strait the next day, anchoring his ships in the open water just outside it. Beyond Yi's 13 combat vessels was a long line of fishing boats packed with refugees. By arranging these vessels in a mock battle line, the admiral hoped that the Japanese would assume his own squadron was merely the vanguard of a larger force. That night, with everything set as he wanted, Yi summoned his commanders to an audience, telling them that "He who seeks death shall live! He who seeks his life shall die!".

At dawn, the next day, the main Japanese armada of two to three hundred vessels approached the southern end of the Myeongnyang Strait. As Yi had predicted, this huge mass of ships was unable to pass through the narrow channel of Myeongnyang in one group, and thus began to split into separate squadrons. Everything was going according to Yi's plan. It was only when the first enemy ships began to emerge into the open water that Yi ordered the attack. The Japanese fleet had not realised the Koreans were there, but were finally notified by the cannons and fire arrows that began to attack them. However, as the admiral's flagship blasted the stunned enemy warships, the other ships in his fleet began to lag behind, witnessing the extraordinary odds they faced. Nevertheless, threats of punishment and Yi's dogged determination motivated his captains to catch up and fight. At this point, the meager 13-ship Korean fleet was completely enveloped by at least 130 Japanese vessels.

Putting Korea's newfound dominance at sea to good use, Admiral Yi tightly blockaded Yukinaga inside Suncheon. Despite Yi's insistence that the Japanese would not be allowed to escape, Yukinaga's diplomatic pressure on the Chinese eventually allowed one ship to escape. This craft then signaled the rest of Japan's wajo naval forces to rendezvous inside the bay at Sacheon, to prepare for the voyage home. After Yukinaga failed to show up, the Japanese forces realised the situation he was in, and sent 500 ships to break the blockade. Informed by scouts and local fishermen as to what was happening, Yi anticipated that the Japanese would take the direct route between Sacheon and Suncheon, through the Noryang strait. He was correct.

Having drawn up his ships in the open sea just west of the narrow strait, a surprise attack was launched at 2am on the 17th of December 1598. Within hours, almost half the Japanese fleet was burned or sunk. Admiral Yi was in the thick of the fighting.

THE AFTERMATH OF THE IMJIN WAR

1600-1636

As the war came to a close, the ramifications of the conflict continued to be felt by all three nations involved. For Japan, the defeat marked a turning point in its history as the country shifted towards a centralized government led by the powerful Tokugawa clan. This new ruling dynasty would go on to rule Japan for over two centuries, solidifying its control over the country and ushering in a period of relative peace and stability.

For the Ming and Joseon dynasties, the war had left both nations weakened and vulnerable to outside invaders. The Ming dynasty, in particular, would eventually fall in 1644 due to a combination of internal rebellion and Manchu intervention. The subsequent Qing dynasty would prove to be a generous overlord to the Koreans, who had managed to maintain their independence despite the war. However, the country would remain isolated and largely cut off from the rest of the world until the late 1800s, when Japan's Imperial restoration would once again bring the two nations into conflict.

The war had a profound impact on all three nations and its effects would be felt for many years to come. The Korean navy, led by the legendary Admiral Yi Sun-shin, had played a crucial role in defending their country and ultimately turning the tide of the war in their favor. But the sacrifices made by the people of all three nations, including the loss of countless lives, would leave a lasting impact on the people and the countries as a whole.

www.ingramcontent.com/pod-product-compliance
Lightning Source LLC
Chambersburg PA
CBHW052117150726
48002CB00006B/2380